My Name is Malia

My Story of Growing Up with a Brother with Special Needs

Julia Gressel-Murray

ISBN 978-1-63814-542-4 (Hardcover)
ISBN 978-1-63814-541-7 (Digital)

Covenant Books
11661 Hwy 707
Murrells Inlet, SC 29576
www.covenantbooks.com

Dedication

Tanya M. my friend, who laid this
book idea on my heart. Thank you.
Malia my daughter, for framing
your vision of your story.
Ben my husband, for loving me
through our life together.

My name is Malia. I am ten years old.

My life is a little different than my friends. I have a little brother who has special needs.

His special needs mean he processes information in a different way. Sometimes he has seizures.

My little brother was born with a condition called hydrocephalus.

It is not an easy word to pronounce. It sounds like this: hi-dro-sef-a-lus.

My brother's name is Tommie. He is seven years old.

I do not know how he ended up being special.

My mom says that God designed him in a special way for a special purpose.

She says, one day we will all see why God chose this condition for Tommie. I cannot wait for that day!

Having a brother who has special needs can be a lot of work. My mom says that my little brother needs a lot of special attention.

Sometimes if I do not play with him, he calls my name over and over. "Malia, Malia, Malia!"

Sometimes I want to play in my room quietly, just me and my Barbies.

My brother loves to play with his plastic dinosaurs. He is able to name the different species of each of them.

He also has memorized all the fifty states! He can tell them all to you in alphabetical order.

I cannot do any of those things. I believe this is part of what makes my little brother so special.

I have learned that having a brother with special needs means sometimes I have to put the things I want to do aside.

My mom says this is called being selfless. That is a good thing. It just means I am being more concerned with my brother's needs than my own.

Once one of my mom's friends said to me, "Being a big sister to a brother with special needs takes a lot of love and patience, and you have both."

Sometimes I wonder if this is why God put him in my life.

At night after we have dinner, Mom gets on the floor with my little brother and plays with him.

I heard my mom say it is important that he gets one-on-one time with her as much as possible.

When I hear my mom talking to Tommie, it makes me happy. At the end of their playtime, she reads a story before tucking him into bed.

Sometimes my mom is too tired to play with me when she comes home from work. She has an awfully long drive home.

I know she works hard every day for me and my brother so she can put food on the table and give us a nice place to live.

So, I am okay playing with my Barbies by myself. I know Tommie needs the extra special attention from my mom.

I know my mom loves me just as much as she loves Tommie.

SUNSHINE DAY CARE

17

After school, Tommie and I go to daycare.

I stay close to my brother because I want to protect him from kids who do not understand that he is special.

I know some kids can be mean and make fun of him. When that happens, I stand up to those bullies.

I will always protect my brother!

19

Being a big sister to a brother with special needs is a lot of responsibility. I know my mom is proud of me because she tells me every day.

My mom can rely on me to help out around the house, especially with chores on Saturdays. I work hard to keep my room clean so that my mom does not have to do extra work.

When I have my friends over to my house to play, I try to think of ways that I can include my little brother.

Barbies and dinosaurs have become a normal way for me, Tommie, and my friends to play together.

My friends have fun making up stories about Barbies and dinosaurs!

I believe this helps my brother learn how to play with other kids, while my friends learn how to play with him.

Many times, when lying in bed at night, I think about what my brother and I will be like when we get older.

Will my little brother live with me when we are big like my mom? Will I be like my mom, working and then coming home to make dinner and spend time with my brother?

Sometimes these questions swirl around in my head. I do not know if other ten-year-olds think about these kinds of things.

All I know is that I will always be my brother's protector, with Barbies and dinosaurs forever!

About the Author

Julia Gressel-Murray lives in San Leandro, California, with her husband, Ben. They are a blended family of six. They have a heart for the special needs community because their youngest sons each have a different special need.

After completing a successful forty plus-year career in the corporate industry, Julia is now a stay-at-home mom caring for her children, who are now in their mid-twenties. She keeps busy as a wife, mother, entrepreneur, and friend. She enjoys creating and making new connections. Her books continue to be a tool she uses to reach, teach, and inspire parents and children alike. She says everyone has their own story that should be told. She looks forward to writing about her stepson with autism and other stories that are close to her heart.

CPSIA information can be obtained
at www.ICGtesting.com
Printed in the USA
LVHW081341120523
746817LV00002B/59